W9-DDT-843

MOTHER JONES
AND THE MARCH OF
THE MILL CHILDREN

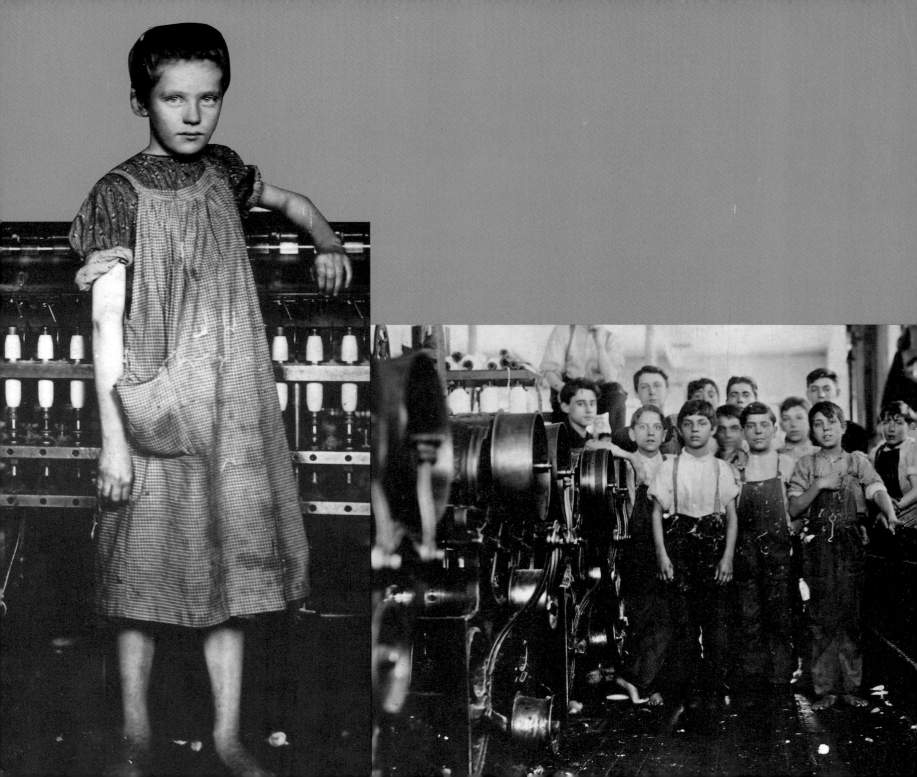

MOTHER JONES AND THE MARCH
OF THE MILL CHILDREN

BY PENNY COLMAN

THE MILLBROOK PRESS
BROOKFIELD, CONNECTICUT

FOR EDA J. LeSHAN,
ANOTHER PASSIONATE FIGHTER
FOR GOOD CAUSES

SPECIAL THANKS TO LINDA HICKSON
AND ELIZABETH M. REIS FOR A
TERRIFIC RESEARCH EXPEDITION

Photo research by Penny Colman

Cover photos courtesy of Bettmann Archive

Photographs courtesy of the Library of Congress: pp. 6, 43; Bettmann Archive: pp. 10, 13, 19, 20, 28; Free Library of Philadelphia: p. 17; *The Philadelphia Inquirer,* June 2, 1903 (photo by Penny Colman): p. 23; *The Comrade*, 1903 (photos by Penny Colman): pp. 25, 36, 41; *The Evening Bulletin*, July 7, 1903 (photo by Penny Colman): p. 27; Archives of Labor and Urban Affairs, Wayne State University: p. 31; Tamiment Institute Library, New York University: pp. 42, 44.

Published by The Millbrook Press
2 Old New Milford Road
Brookfield, Connecticut 06804

Library of Congress
Cataloging-in-Publication Data
Colman, Penny
Mother Jones and the march of the mill
children / by Penny Colman.
p. cm.
Includes bibliographical references and index.
ISBN 1-56294-402-9 (lib. bdg.)
1. Jones, Mother, 1843?-1930—Juvenile
literature.   2. Women in the labor
movement—United States—Biography—
Juvenile literature.   3. Women social
reformers—United States—History—Juvenile
literature.   4. Children—Employment—
United States—History—Juvenile literature.
[1. Jones, Mother, 1843?-1930. 2.
Reformers. 3. Children—Employment—
History.] I. Title.
HD8073.J6C64 1994   331.88'092—
dc20 [B]   93-1933 CIP AC

MOTHER JONES
AND THE MARCH OF
THE MILL CHILDREN

The *"hell-raiser"* appears next to
one of her sayings on this poster.

MARY
HARRIS
JONES was called a lot of names. "Agitator . . . fanatic . . . the most dangerous woman in America," said some people. "Angel . . . champion . . . a great humanitarian," said others. "Get it right," Jones herself said, "I'm a hell-raiser." Jones didn't start out as a hell-raiser. In fact, she didn't become one until she was about forty years old and had suffered terrible tragedies.

Jones fought for the rights of miners, railroad workers, and mill and factory workers. When employers hired poor children to work in those dangerous jobs, a common practice, Jones fought extra hard. In 1903 she led a twenty-day protest march against child labor some 125 miles (200 kilometers) to see the president of the United States. Mill children and adult workers marched with Jones, and stories about the march appeared in newspapers every day. This is the story of that historic march and the hell-raiser who led it.

———

Mary Harris Jones was born in County Cork, Ireland. Although there are no records to prove it, Jones always claimed that she was born on May 1, 1830. When she was about seven years old, Jones, who was known then as Mary Harris, and her family left Ireland and moved to Toronto, Canada. Her father worked for the railroad, and her mother took care of the family. Mary loved learning things, and her parents made sure that she went to school, even though many people at that time thought that girls didn't need to. Mary Harris got a good education, and when she finished school she became a teacher in Monroe, Michigan. Then she worked as a dressmaker in Chicago, Illinois, for a time, before deciding to return to teaching. It was while she was a teacher in Memphis, Tennessee, that she met George E. Jones.

George Jones was an ironmolder and an active member of the Iron Molders Union, a group of ironworkers who formed a union so that they could pressure employers to provide better working conditions and pay better wages. Because of George, Mary learned a lot about unions and became friends with other union members. She also saw how workers lived with very little money, and employers lived with a lot.

Mary and George got married in 1861, the same year that the Civil War began. Throughout the war, they were busy earning a living, helping the Iron Molders Union, and raising their four children. In 1867, two years after the Civil War ended, a terrible tragedy tore the Jones family apart. Years later, Mary Harris Jones described what happened in her autobiography:

In 1867 a yellow fever epidemic swept Memphis. Its victims were mainly among the poor and the workers. The rich and the well-to-do fled the city. . . . The dead surrounded us. They were buried at night quickly and without ceremony. All about my house I could hear weeping and the cries of delirium. One by one, my four little children sickened and died. I washed their little bodies and got them ready for burial. My husband caught the fever and died. I sat alone through nights of grief. No one came to me. No one could. Other homes were as stricken as was mine. All day long, all night long, I heard the grating of the wheels of the death cart.

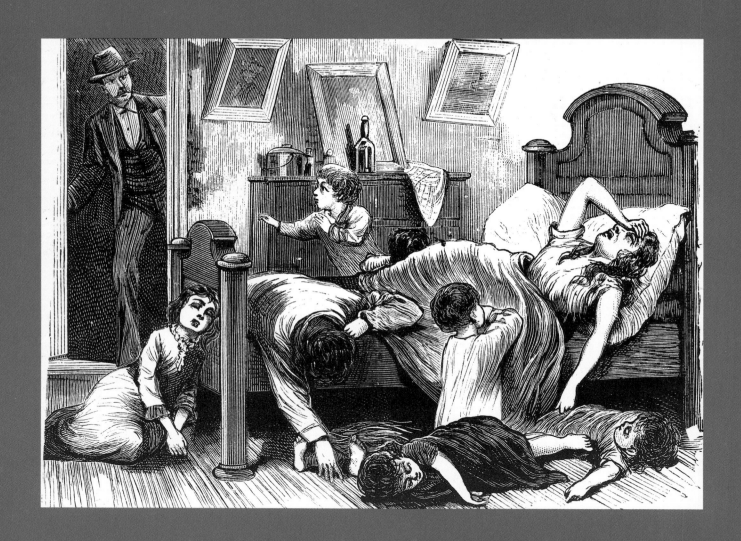

Mary Harris Jones buried her four children and husband. Then she nursed other yellow fever victims. After the epidemic ended, she moved back to Chicago and started working again as a dressmaker. Carrying her needle, thread, scissors, and material, Jones went to the homes of rich people to sew their fancy clothes. She was distressed by the difference between the rich and the poor. "Often while sewing for the lords and barons who lived in magnificent houses . . . I would look out of the plate glass windows and see the poor, shivering wretches, jobless and hungry," she wrote. "The contrast of their condition . . . was painful to me. My employers seemed neither to notice nor to care."

In 1871, Mary Harris Jones suffered another tragedy when a fire swept through Chicago. Known as the Great Fire, it burned for a day and a night with flames like the winds of a hurricane destroying everything they touched. Hundreds of people died, thousands of people lost their homes, and more than 17,450 buildings were burned to the ground. Except for her life and the clothes she was wearing, Mary Harris Jones lost everything in the Great Fire.

In the devastated city, Jones found comfort "in an old, tumbled down, fire scorched building" where the Noble Or-

Facing page: Yellow fever epidemics broke out in Memphis several times. This engraving shows a family stricken with the disease in 1879.

der of the Knights of Labor met. Founded in Philadelphia in 1869, the Knights of Labor was a nationwide labor organization that helped workers improve their lives.

Industrial workers lived hard lives. The hours were long, usually eleven to twelve hours a day, six days a week. The wages were low, about $1 to $1.25 a day for unskilled male workers, $2 a day for skilled male workers, and $2 to $4 a week for women and children. The working conditions were dirty and dangerous with poor lighting, little ventilation or sanitation, and no safety devices on the machines.

Employers owned the stores where the workers shopped and the houses—shacks really—where they lived. And the owners didn't hesitate to charge high prices for food, supplies, and rent and to deduct the money from the workers' paychecks. One railroad worker framed the weekly paycheck he got; after all the company deductions, the paycheck was for two cents. "There is no limit to which powers of privilege will not go to keep the workers in slavery," Jones said.

In an effort to protect themselves, more and more workers joined unions like the Knights of Labor with the hope that they could accomplish more as a group. Unions used a variety of tactics to pressure employers, including

declaring a strike. During a strike, workers refused to work until their demands were accepted. Employers used a variety of tactics to break a strike, such as hiring new workers, who the strikers called "scabs" or "strikebreakers."

The Knights of Labor members welcomed Mary Harris Jones. She attended their meetings and listened to labor leaders describe the miserable lives that workers lived. Jones was outraged: "Poor men and women and little children worked from morning to night for bread, nothing but bread, no hope of anything better, only the opportunity to prolong their miserable lives."

Jones identified with the workers. Her father had been a railroad worker and her husband had been an ironworker. "I belong to a class who has been robbed, exploited, and plundered down through the many long centuries and because I belong to that class I have the instinct to go and break the chains," she explained. And, thus, Mary Harris Jones became a "hell-raiser." She traveled to coal mines, railroad yards, factories, and mills from Cabin Creek, West Virginia, to Ludlow, Colorado; from Roaring Branch, Pennsylvania, to Birmingham, Alabama. "My address is like my shoes: it travels with me," Jones wrote. "I abide where there is a fight against wrong."

Mary Harris Jones agitated, organized, and encouraged workers. "My life's work has been to educate the worker to a sense of the wrongs he has had to suffer, and does suffer," she explained, "and to stir up the oppressed to a point of getting off their knees and demanding that which I believe to be rightfully theirs."

Labor disputes were frequently violent. Employers hired private detectives and thugs to intimidate workers, and they brought in scabs to take the strikers' jobs. Both sides shouted threats, accusations, and ugly words. Strikers were beaten up, and they responded by chasing away the scabs. Property was damaged and destroyed. Local police, state militia, and federal troops moved in to restore order. All too often people were injured or killed—police officers, innocent bystanders, and workers.

Jones was fearless. "I am not afraid of the pen, the sword or scaffold. I will tell the truth," she said, "wherever I please." She also wasn't afraid of jail, which was good since she was repeatedly arrested and thrown in jail for holding meetings and leading protest marches or disobeying a court order that forbade such activities. "Goodbye, boys. I'm under arrest. Keep up the fight! Don't surrender," she shouted to a group of striking miners as the police took her away. Her "boys," the men who worked in the mines, mills, and factories, called her "Mother." So did the women and children workers. Soon almost everyone who met her called her Mother Jones.

As if in uniform, Mother Jones usually wore a long, full black skirt and a black blouse with lace tucked around the neckline. She was about 5 feet (150 centimeters) tall and had a solid, trim body. Her eyes were deep-set, small, and sparkling blue. Her full lips, which she pressed tightly together, were red against her white skin. Her hair was even whiter than her skin. People who heard her speak remembered her voice—intense, powerful, and rhythmic. According to one listener, when Jones spoke, "suddenly everyone sat up alert and listened."

———

About 1894, Mother Jones got a job in a cotton mill in Cottondale, Alabama. "I wanted to see for myself if the grewsome [gruesome] stories of little children working in the mills were true," she wrote in her autobiography. The manager of the mill refused to hire her unless she "had a family that would work also." Jones lied and said that she had six children who would be coming to join her soon. The manager eagerly hired her and showed her a house for rent.

Mother Jones in her "uniform."

Facing page: Young workers in a Georgia cotton mill. Like the children Mother Jones wrote about, they tended machines and replaced spindles of thread.

"The house he brought me to was a sort of two-story plank shanty. The windows were broken and the door sagged open. Its latch was broken. It had one room downstairs and an unfinished loft upstairs. Through the cracks in the roof the rain had come in and rotted the flooring. Downstairs there was a big old open fireplace in front of which were holes big enough to drop a brick through," she wrote.

According to Jones, the manager was "delighted with the house." When she pointed out that the wind and the cold would come through the holes, the manager laughed and said, "Oh, it will be summer soon and you will need all the air you can get."

Jones rented the house and reported to work in the cotton mill. She saw for herself that the stories were true:

Little girls and boys, barefooted, walked up and down between the endless rows of spindles, reaching thin little hands into the machinery to repair snapped threads. They crawled under machinery to oil it. They replaced spindles all day long [and all] night through. Tiny babies of six years old with faces of sixty did an eight-hour shift for ten cents a day. If they fell asleep, cold water was dashed in their faces, and the voice of the manager yelled above the ceaseless racket

and whir of the machines. Toddling chaps of four years old were brought to the mills to "help" the older sister or brother of ten years but their labor was not paid.

When the manager grew suspicious because Jones's six children didn't show up, she left Cottondale and got a job in a rope factory in Tuscaloosa: "This factory was run also by child labor. The machinery needed constant cleaning. The tiny, slender bodies of the little children crawled in and about under dangerous machinery, oiling and cleaning. Often their hands were crushed. A finger was snapped off."

Child labor in America was nothing new. Children had always worked. During colonial times, children worked alongside their parents, on farms and in home industries such as weaving and candlemaking. As machines were invented and factories and mills were built, children worked there, too.

In 1789, when Samuel Slater built the first cotton-spinning mill in America, among the millworkers he hired were nine children under the age of twelve. One advertisement for workers at Slater's mill read: "They [the mill owners] wish to hire . . . a Family, of from five to eight children, capable of working in a Cotton Mill." Within ten years, a hundred children between the ages of four and ten were

Facing page: The children working at this spinning machine are covered with fuzz and dirt. Conditions in many factories at this time were poor.

working in Slater's mill. Employers liked to hire children because they could be paid lower wages, were easier to control, and were not likely to form or join labor unions.

By 1900 an estimated 2,250,000 children under the age of sixteen worked in various industries. The textile industry, the mills and factories that spun cotton and wove wool into such goods as sweaters, rugs, knit hats, and horse blankets, employed the greatest number of children. Some states had child labor laws, which set a minimum age at which a child could be hired and the maximum number of hours the child could work per day. Generally, the minimum age was twelve and the maximum hours were ten a day. But these laws were rarely enforced. Because workers' families desperately needed their wages, many children lied about their age. So did their parents, who would buy fake certificates to "prove" that their child was old enough to work. In addition to needing their children's wages, parents knew that they would probably lose their jobs or be evicted from their company-owned houses if their children didn't work.

———

Mother Jones was determined to do something about child labor, or "child slavery," as she called it. In 1903, at the age of seventy-three, Jones went to Philadelphia, Pennsylvania, where 100,000 textile workers including 16,000 children were on strike. The strike had been called by the Central Textile Workers' Union after mill owners refused to shorten the workweek from sixty hours to fifty-five.

The union leaders were particularly concerned about the effects of the long hours on children workers. "Long and incessant toil ruins their health. . . . The textile industry of Philadelphia rests on the bowed backs of young and helpless children," they said. The union was so concerned that all the workers were willing to take a cut in pay to get a fifty-five-hour workweek. (Today a workweek is forty hours.) But the owners refused. They said they couldn't afford it. So, workers at six hundred textile mills went on strike.

The union headquarters were in the Labor Lyceum, a building located at Second and Cambria streets in Kensington, Pennsylvania, a section of Philadelphia. Mother Jones spent long hours there organizing the workers. She participated in mass meetings, parades, picnics, and peaceful demonstrations. She also talked to the children. "Every day little children came into Union Headquarters, some with their hands off, some with the thumb missing, some with their fingers off at the knuckle. They were stooped little things, round shoul-

A headline from The Philadelphia Inquirer *reporting the textile strike on June 2, 1903.*

dered and skinny," Mother Jones wrote. She asked newspaper reporters why they weren't writing "the facts about child labor." The reporters told her that the mill owners had stock in the newspapers and controlled what the papers published. "Well, I've got stock in these children, and I'll arrange a little publicity," Mother Jones replied.

On June 17, 1903, Mother Jones started getting publicity with a large demonstration at City Hall. "I put the little boys with their fingers off and hands crushed and maimed on a platform. I held up their mutilated hands and showed them to the crowd and made the statement that Philadelphia's mansions were built on the broken bones, the quivering hearts and drooping heads of these little children." She held up the children so city officials standing in their open office windows could see them and "pointed to their puny arms and legs and hollow chests." Jones talked about children being "sacrificed on the altar of profit" and about "millionaire manufacturers" who commit "moral murders."

Because of the size of the demonstration and Jones's dramatic speech, the newspapers published a report of the event. "That was what I wanted. Public attention on the subject of child labor," Jones wrote. But the attention did not

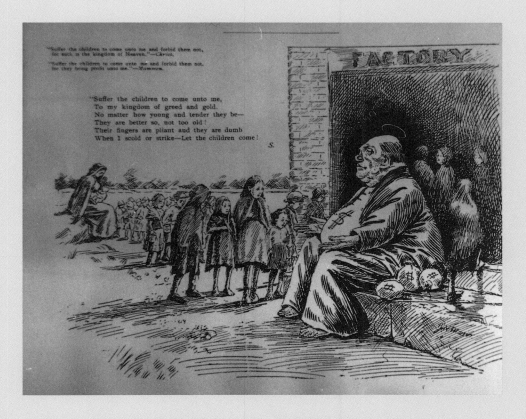

In this 1903 cartoon, children trudge past a greedy "angel" of profit into a factory. The cartoon is based on the Biblical saying: "You cannot serve God and mammon." Mammon means wealth, and the cartoon implies that factory owners serve it—at children's expense.

last long, so Jones "concluded that people needed stirring up again."

Jones knew that the Liberty Bell, the bell that rang in Philadelphia when the Declaration of Independence was announced in 1776, was on a popular tour around the country. Crowds of people came out to see it. "That gave me an idea. These little children were striking for some of the freedom," Jones wrote, "and I decided that the children and I would go on a tour." Jones's plan was to march mill children some 125 miles (200 kilometers) to visit the president of the United States, Theodore Roosevelt, at his summer home in Oyster Bay on Long Island, just outside of New York City. Jones intended to ask Roosevelt to urge Congress to pass a law prohibiting child labor: "I thought that President Roosevelt might see these mill children and compare them with his own little ones who were spending the summer on the seashore."

On July 5, 1903, Mother Jones spoke at a huge meeting for strikers. She told them about her plan and assured the parents that she would bring their children back "safe and sound." The strikers voted to support her, and by July 7, Mother Jones and her army, as it was being called, were ready to march.

———

"As gaily as though they were going on a grand picnic, a strange little army of textile workers marched from Kensington this afternoon. At the head of the column was a gray-haired woman, middle-aged man and a wee bit of a boy," a newspaper reporter wrote. Of course, Mother Jones was the "gray-haired woman." The middle-aged man was Charles Sweeney, the chief marshal of Jones's army. He twirled a red, white, and blue baton as he marched. The boy was Danny Thomas, an eight-year-old worker who carried a sign with the words, "We Are Textile Workers." Other children carried American flags and signs. One sign read, "We want time to play." Another read, "We only ask for Justice."

There were almost three hundred marchers, nearly two hundred of them young children, in Jones's army. The rest were adult textile workers. They were accompanied by a fife-and-drum corps that played "Marching Through Georgia." Four wagons rattled along behind the army. Three wagons carried supplies, including a wash boiler, or huge pot for cooking their food, and tents. The other wagon was for children who needed a ride. Each child carried a knife, fork, tin cup, and plate in a knapsack.

Jones and her army were headed for Torresdale Park, 12 miles (20 kilometers) away, where they planned to spend the

MOTHER JONES OFF WITH A LITTLE ARMY

Young "Crusaders" from Textile Mills, 300 Strong, Start on the March to New York.

LED BY FIFE AND DRUM

As gaily as though they were going on a grand picnic for the balance of the day, a strange little army of textile workers marched from Kensington this afternoon. At the head of the column was a gray-haired woman, a middle-aged man and a wee bit of a boy. They reminded one of that stirring picture, "The Spirit of '76," and the struggling band of men and boys behind them began their march with much the same impulse that inspired the colonial army of America in its battle for freedom. The odd procession to-day was one of the features of the struggle now being waged in the textile world, and its object was to create sympathy for the toilers and sentiment in favor of their battle, as well as gain funds to carry on the fight.

The newspaper article that dubbed Mother Jones's marchers "a strange little army."

Members of Mother Jones's army and their signs.

first night. It was a hot, dry, dusty July day. After a few miles, Jones put the girls on a trolley car that went to the park, and she climbed aboard a wagon and rode with some of the small boys. By six o'clock all the marchers reached Torresdale Park. After a supper of bread and cheese and fruits and vegetables donated by local farmers, Mother Jones spoke to a crowd of a thousand people. When she asked for donations, the spectators donated $76.40 to the strike fund.

Determined not to have any trouble, Jones gave her marchers strict orders—no one was to loot or to enter or leave camp after ten o'clock at night. She quickly dismissed a man and a boy who jumped a fence and chased some chickens. She also sent home three eleven-year-old boys who did not have their parents' permission to march. Other marchers left for a variety of reasons, including fatigue. According to a newspaper report, by the end of the first day, "180 men, 20 girls, 10 boys, and 8 women answered the roll call."

On July 8 the army had sandwiches, coffee, and ice cream for breakfast. Then, according to a newspaper report, the army "left Torresdale at 9 A.M. after Mother Jones and Sweeney weeded out another 150 marchers—hangers-on, young women who were sent home for fear their reputations might be attacked, and thin-faced boys and girls who could

Facing page: Mother Jones and her young crusaders on the move. The army stopped several times for Jones to make speeches.

not stand the rigors of the march. Then off through the dust-laden road went the depleted army led by the band."

The army planned to stay in Bristol, Pennsylvania, but police officers stopped them at the Otter Creek Bridge that led into Bristol. It seemed that the owners of a large textile mill in Bristol and the town officials were worried that Mother Jones would cause trouble. When Jones assured them that she would cause no "disorder," the officials agreed to let the army cross the bridge. But first, the marchers rested along the banks of Otter Creek and ate a meal of condensed soup, canned corned beef, bread and butter, and coffee. According to a newspaper report, the "hot water for the soup and ice for the water were given by a fireman at the Bristol ice plant and Farmer Slack gave the coffee and cooked the meal. Ed Hinkle-smith [the marcher in charge of food supplies], returning [from Bristol] on his bicycle with a bag of salt ran into a wagon. The salt was lost and the soup went unseasoned."

Two thousand people attended Mother Jones's speech that night in Bristol, including "not only the local textile workers but the better people of the town as well," wrote a reporter. According to the reporter, the "cold curiosity of the audience changed to intense interest and approval. Particularly . . . when Mother Jones denounced child slavery in the

mills." Mrs. Jennie Silbert, the proprietor of the hotel, invited Mrs. Jones, five women, two little girls and any little boys who were ill to stay at her hotel. The rest of the marchers camped out in a vacant lot at Mill and Pond streets. On the next morning, July 9, the army left for Morrisville, Pennsylvania, where they planned to spend the night before marching across the Delaware River Bridge and entering Trenton, New Jersey.

———

"Mother Jones and Her Army at the New Jersey Bridge," read the headline in the *New York Tribune*. A reporter visited Mother Jones's camp and found "about 60 men and boys lying under trees waiting for vegetable soup which was cooking over a wood fire in a huge copper wash boiler. They had gone swimming in the afternoon and washed their clothes. Close by the rude outdoor kitchen was a pyramid of tin cups in which the soup was to be served while against a large tree leaned the banners and numerous United States flags which are carried." The reporter also visited Mother Jones. "Our crusade is chiefly against child labor in the mills. Give the young girls of the workingman's family a chance to learn something and be something," she told him.

On July 10, Jones and her army crossed the Delaware River Bridge. But first they had to pay a toll of two cents per person. Mother Jones strongly objected to having to pay a toll to the "unfeeling corporation" that operated the bridge. Bridges should be free, she told the bridge-keeper. Then she paid $1.04 for herself and the fifty-one marchers left in her army. That night in Trenton, Jones spoke to about five thousand people: "The army I'm leading on to New York is composed of intelligent workmen. . . . Our cause is a just one and we propose to show the New York millionaires our grievances."

Mother Jones, the other women, and children spent the night in the homes of labor leaders. The men stayed with "Glad Hand" Tom Terradell, a rich man who ran a free lodging house for hoboes. On the next morning, July 11, they left for Princeton, New Jersey. About noon, a severe thunderstorm struck. Drenched and chilled, the marchers found shelter in a barn that they discovered belonged to former president Grover Cleveland. Although Cleveland was away, his caretaker invited the marchers to spend the night. But the rain ended soon, and Jones decided to go on to Princeton where a newspaper reporter discovered she "was not in a cheerful mood."

A professor at Princeton University invited Jones to speak to his economics class. She accepted and took ten-year-old James Ashworth with her. Pointing to Ashworth, Jones told the college students, "He is stooped over because his spine is curved from carrying, day after day, bundles of yarn that weigh seventy-five pounds. He gets three dollars a week and his sister, who is fourteen, gets six dollars. They work in a carpet factory ten hours a day while the children of the rich are getting their higher education."

Jones did not spend the night in Princeton but rode by train with her army to Highland Park, New Jersey, a town across the Raritan River from New Brunswick. The fife-and-drum corps gave concerts on various street corners and passed the hat hoping for donations. As usual, Jones spoke: "Today we are making more millionaires in a week than they did in three centuries years ago. We murder more children in a week in factories, mills, and mines than are killed in the armies of the world. What will be the generation of the future?" she asked.

The army, now down to about forty-one marchers, as people continued to drop out from fatigue, spent two nights, July 11 and 12, in Highland Park. It was a miserable time. Another thunderstorm struck. "When the rain had finished, mosquitoes made a raid upon the camp," a newspaper reporter wrote. Some of the marchers left camp and took the train back to Philadelphia.

Mother Jones and her remaining marchers kept going. Crowds of people welcomed her army at each stop and donated food and money. Newspapers in the towns along the way printed articles. So did the major newspapers in New York City and Philadelphia. On July 13 the marchers stayed in Metuchen, New Jersey. The next day they went to Rahway, where Mother Jones had arranged for the army to spend the night in the Rahway Inn. They slept on the floor there in a large room.

On July 15, Jones and her army arrived in Elizabeth, New Jersey, where the press heralded her as "the greatest female agitator in the country . . . an intelligent woman, a great thinker, and a forceful speaker." The army spent two days in Elizabeth. The workers in Elizabeth entertained the marchers and raised money for them. Saloon keepers offered them free beer, but Mother Jones ordered her marchers to refuse the offer. Two businessmen took Mother Jones on her first automobile ride. While she was in Elizabeth, Jones sent a letter to Theodore Roosevelt: "We ask you, Mr. President, if our commercial greatness has not cost us too much by being built

This photo shows a handful of young marchers and two adults. As the march progressed, many dropped out.

upon the quivering hearts of helpless children. We who know of these sufferings have taken up their cause and are now marching toward you in the hope that your tender heart will counsel with us to abolish this crime."

On July 17 the army spent the night in Newark. The next two nights they were in Paterson, then on to Passaic on July 20, where Jones discovered the president's Secret Service had been following the army. In fact, two agents stayed in the hotel room next to hers in Passaic and took turns spying on her through the keyhole of the connecting doors. On July 21, the army camped in West Hoboken. The next day they stayed in Jersey City Heights and had their last campfire before crossing the Hudson River and entering New York City.

———

Entering New York City wasn't easy. The police commissioner refused to give Jones a parade permit. "Then I'll go to the Mayor," Jones replied. She reminded the mayor he had recently given parade permits to a German prince and a Chinese dignitary. Surely, he could give one to "workers in textile factories who are trying to show the world what they are suffering." And with that, the mayor gave in and Mother Jones got her permit.

On July 23, Jones and her army crossed the Hudson River on the Christopher Street Ferry. That night they marched up Second Avenue from East 4th Street to 27th Street and Madison Avenue. Police officers lined the route, and thousands of people cheered as the marchers played their fifes and drums, clanged cymbals, carried their signs high, and waved the American flag. At the intersection of 27th Street and Madison, Mother Jones climbed aboard a wagon draped in red. With her arms around three eleven-year-old mill children—Gussie Rangnew, Joseph Ashford, and Eddie Dunphy—Jones spoke to a crowd of about 30,000 people: "We are marching quietly to the President's home. I believe he can do something for these children," she said. "He surely could tell Congress to pass a bill that would take the children out of the God-accursed mills and put them into the schools."

Jones and her army stayed in New York for several days. They went to Coney Island as guests of Frank Bostock, the owner of a wild animal show. Standing on a board resting on two chairs in front of the animal cages, Mother Jones spoke to a large crowd. A reporter wrote: "She had barely begun to talk when the largest lion . . . set up a horrible roar, the others joining in. During her remarks, Mother Jones was constantly interrupted by the discourteous beasts." Undeterred, Mother

Jones talked at length. At one point she said, "The trouble is that the fellers in Washington don't care. I saw them last Winter pass three railroad bills in one hour, but when labor cries for aid for the little ones, they turn their backs and will not listen. I asked a man in prison once how he happened to get there. He had stolen a pair of shoes. I told him that if he had stolen a railroad he could be a United States Senator."

Finally, on July 27, Mother Jones boarded a train for Oyster Bay. She took only three children and two union men and their wives. No one recognized her when they got off the train and walked the short distance to Roosevelt's beautiful home. Roosevelt's secretary, Benjamin F. Barnes, met them. The president "has nothing to do with such matters and could not assist her 'children' in their struggle for better conditions," he told Mother Jones. Barnes went on to suggest that she write another letter to Roosevelt. Jones and her group took the next train back to New York City. "I have been moved to this crusade, Mr. President, because of actual experience in the mills. I feel that no nation can be truly great while such conditions exist without attempting a remedy," Jones wrote to Roosevelt. She begged him to see "three boys who have walked a hundred miles, serving as living proof of what I say."

On August 4, Jones received a letter from Barnes telling her that she had Roosevelt's "heartiest sympathy with every effort to prevent child labor in factories." But, the letter continued, the laws needed to be passed by the individual states, not the federal government, so there was nothing that Roosevelt could do. Clearly, the president wasn't going to see Mother Jones and her mill children.

That same day, Jones and her remaining marchers took the train back to Philadelphia. "The president refused to see us," she wrote, "but our march had done its work. We had drawn the attention of the nation to the crime of child labor."

———

Mother Jones was right. More people started to talk about child labor. Professors, politicians, and the press spoke out against it. So did religious leaders. In 1905 the Pennsylvania legislature passed a child labor law that "sent thousands of children home from the mills, and kept thousands of others from entering the factory," Jones reported. State after state passed similar laws. Eventually, in 1938, a federal child labor law was passed.

Not long after Jones's return to Philadelphia, the textile workers ran out of money and had to return to work for sixty

The Strenuous Situation at Oyster Bay

"I see you, Mr. President."

"But I saw you first, Mother Jones."

—Philadelphia Evening Telegram.

This cartoon shows President Roosevelt fleeing Mother Jones.

Mother Jones marching with striking workers in Michigan in 1913.

hours a week. The strike was over and the workers had lost, but the union continued to fight for improvements.

Mother Jones moved on to help workers in other parts of the country. For another twenty-five years, she agitated, organized, and encouraged workers. Finally on November 30, 1930, Mary Harris "Mother" Jones died. She had lived one hundred years. And for more than half of those years, Mary Harris "Mother" Jones was the best "hell-raiser" in America.

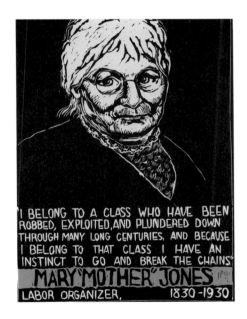

"I BELONG TO A CLASS WHO HAVE BEEN ROBBED, EXPLOITED, AND PLUNDERED DOWN THROUGH MANY LONG CENTURIES, AND BECAUSE I BELONG TO THAT CLASS I HAVE AN INSTINCT TO GO AND BREAK THE CHAINS"
MARY "MOTHER" JONES
LABOR ORGANIZER,   1830-1930

MARY HARRIS "MOTHER"
JONES (1830-1930) Labor Cru-
sader. Toiled mainly among the
miners; but wherever exploitation
was fiercest, there "Mother
Jones" would be found, leading
the fight against oppression and
cheering the workers on.

IMPORTANT DATES

1830? Mary Harris "Mother" Jones is born in Cork, Ireland, probably on May 1.

1867 Jones's four children and husband die in a yellow fever epidemic in Memphis, Tennessee.

1871 Jones loses all her belongings in the Great Fire that swept Chicago.

1877 Mother Jones goes to Pittsburgh to support striking railroad workers and begins her crusade as a "hell-raiser" for working people.

1903 July 7: Mother Jones and her "army" begin their march.

July 27: Mother Jones and three young marchers arrive in Oyster Bay, New York, to meet President Theodore Roosevelt, who refuses to see them.

August 4: Mother Jones returns to Philadelphia.

1904 The National Child Labor Committee is organized to reform child labor.

1905 Pennsylvania passes a child labor law.

1930 Mother Jones dies on November 30 in Hyattsville, Maryland.

1938 Congress passes the Fair Labor Standards Act, which sets some limitations on child labor.

1949 Congress finally passes an amendment to the Fair Labor Standards Act that directly prohibits child labor.

FIND OUT MORE
ABOUT MOTHER JONES

Books

Bethell, Jean.
Three Cheers for Mother Jones!
New York: Holt, Rinehart,
and Winston, 1980.

Rappaport, Doreen.
Trouble at the Mines.
New York: Crowell, 1987.

Poster

For a poster of Mother Jones
write to:

Organization for
Equal Education of the Sexes
P.O. Box 438
Blue Hill, Maine 04614

Places

Here are some places to visit and
numbers to call for information:

Labor Hall of Fame
Frances Perkins Building
Department of Labor
200 Constitution Avenue N.W.
Washington, D.C.
(202) 371-6422

Mother Jones Monument
Union Miners' Cemetery
Mount Olive, Illinois

The National Women's Hall of Fame
76 Fall Street
Seneca Falls, New York
(915) 568-2936

INDEX

Page numbers in *italics* refer to illustrations.

Ashford, Joseph, 38
Ashworth, James, 34

Barnes, Benjamin F., 39, 40
Bostock, Frank, 38
Bristol, Pennsylvania, 30, 32

Central Textile Workers' Union, 23
Chicago, Illinois, 8, 11
Child labor, 16, 18, *19*, *20*, 21–24, *25*
    laws, 22, 26, 40
Civil War, 9
Cleveland, Grover, 33
Colonial period, 21
Cottondale, Alabama, 16
Cotton mills, 16, 18, *19*, *20*, 21–22
County Cork, Ireland, 8

Delaware River Bridge, 32, 33
Dunphy, Eddie, 38

Elizabeth, New Jersey, 35

Factory workers, 7, 12, 14

Great Fire of 1871, 11, *13*

Highland Park, New Jersey, 34
Hinklesmith, Ed, 30

Iron Molders Union, 8, 9

Jersey City Heights, New Jersey, 37
Jones, George E., 8–9
Jones, Mary Harris "Mother," *6*, *17*
    birth of, 8
    child labor and, 7, 16, 18, 21–24
    death of, 43

Jones, Mary Harris "Mother" (*cont.*)
    death of husband and children,
        9, 11
    as dressmaker, 8, 11
    education of, 8
    Great Fire of 1871 and, 11
    in jail, 15
    march to President Roosevelt, 7,
        26–27, *27*, *28*, 29–30, *31*,
        32–35, *36*, 37–40
    marriage of, 9
    nickname of, 16
    physical appearance of, 16
    as teacher, 8
    textile strike of 1903 and, 23–24
    as worker in cotton mill, 16, 18,
        21

Knights of Labor, 12, 14

Liberty Bell, 26

Memphis, Tennessee, 9
Metuchen, New Jersey, 35
Mill workers, 7, 14, 16, 18, 21
Miners, 7, 14–16
Minimum age, 22
Morrisville, Pennsylvania, 32

Newark, New Jersey, 37
Newspapers, 24, 35
New York City, 37–38
New York Tribune, 32

Oyster Bay, New York, 26, 39

Passaic, New Jersey, 37
Princeton, New Jersey, 33–34

Rahway, New Jersey, 35
Railroad workers, 7, 12, 14
Rangnew, Gussie, 38
Roosevelt, Theodore, 26, 35, 38–40,
    41

Scabs (strikebreakers), 14, 15
Silbert, Jennie, 32
Slater, Samuel, 21–22
Strikes, 14, 23–24, 26, 40, 43
Sweeney, Charles, 27, 29

Terradell, Tom, 33
Textile strike of 1903, 23–24, 26, 40,
    43
Thomas, Danny, 27
Torresdale Park, Pennsylvania, 27, 29
Trenton, New Jersey, 32, 33
Tuscaloosa, Alabama, 21

Unions, 8–9, 12, 14, 15, 23

Wages, 8, 12, 18, 22, 23, 34
West Hoboken, New Jersey, 37
Working conditions, 12, 18
Workweek, 12, 22, 23

Yellow fever epidemic, 9, *10*, 11

ABOUT
THE AUTHOR

Penny Colman writes about people who share her commitment to improving the world. She has many books to her credit, including *Breaking the Chains: The Story of Dorothea Dix; Spies! Women in the Civil War; Fannie Lou Hamer and the Fight for the Vote; Madam C. J. Walker: Building a Business Empire;* and *A Woman Unafraid: The Achievements of Francis Perkins.*

When Colman is not traveling to appear as a guest speaker on any number of topics, she lives in Englewood, New Jersey, where she is an active member of the school board.